THE
SERENGETI
MIGRATION

Africa's Animals on the Move

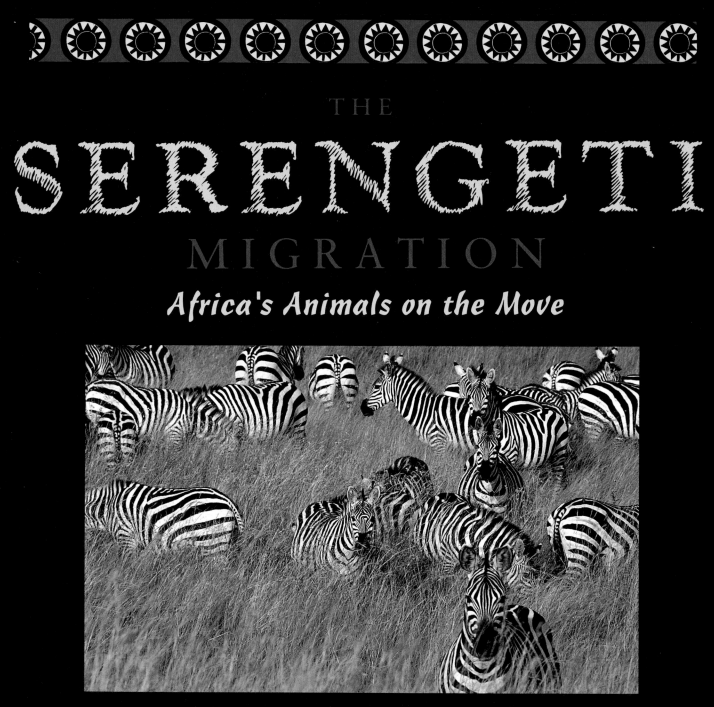

Lisa Lindblad

Photography by **Sven-Olof Lindblad**

Hyperion Books for Children
New York

For Justin and Jeremy: You always make this ancient land look new.

For more information address Hyperion Books for Children,
114 Fifth Avenue, New York, New York 10011.
Photographs on pages 36, 37, and 41 are courtesy of Planet Earth Pictures.

First Edition
1 3 5 7 9 10 8 6 4 2

Library of Congress Cataloging-in-Publication Data
Lindblad, Lisa.
The Serengeti migration / by Lisa Lindblad; photographs by Sven-Olof Lindblad.—1st ed.
p. cm.
ISBN 1-56282-668-9 (trade).—ISBN 1-56282-669-7 (library)
1. Gnus—Tanzania—Serengeti National Park—Migration—Juvenile
literature.   2. Zebras—Tanzania—Serengeti National Park—
Migration—Juvenile literature.   3. Serengeti National Park
(Tanzania) [1. Gnus—Migration.   2. Zebras—Migration.
3. Serengeti National Park (Tanzania) 4. National parks and
reserves—Tanzania.] I. Lindblad, Sven-Olof, ill. II. Title.
QL737.U53L55 1994 599.73′58—dc20 93-26338 CIP AC

The decorative motif used throughout the design of this book was created by repeating
a detail taken from a hammered wire design on a wooden stool made by the Kamba tribe of Kenya.

THE
SERENGETI
MIGRATION
Africa's Animals on the Move

The Serengeti National Park Conservation Area

A conservation area is set aside to protect and manage the land and its animal and plant life.   The Serengeti National Park is part of a large conservation area that crosses the boundaries of two countries, Tanzania and Kenya, in East Africa. The entire area consists of the Serengeti, the Maasai Mara Game Reserve, the Maswa Game Reserve, and the Ngorongoro Conservation Area.

The migration of wildebeests and zebras usually begins in the Ngorongoro Conservation Area but the majority of the journey occurs within the Serengeti National Park. The detail map on the facing page shows the migration as described in this book. However, the exact route the animals take changes each year as it is dependent on when the rains begin and where they fall.

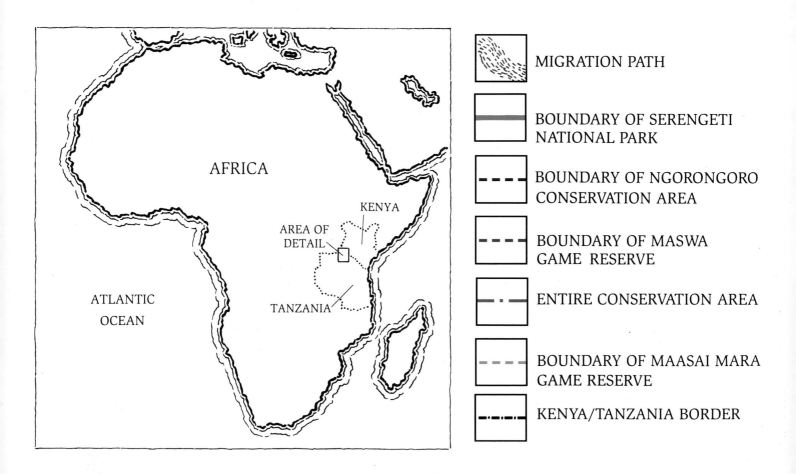

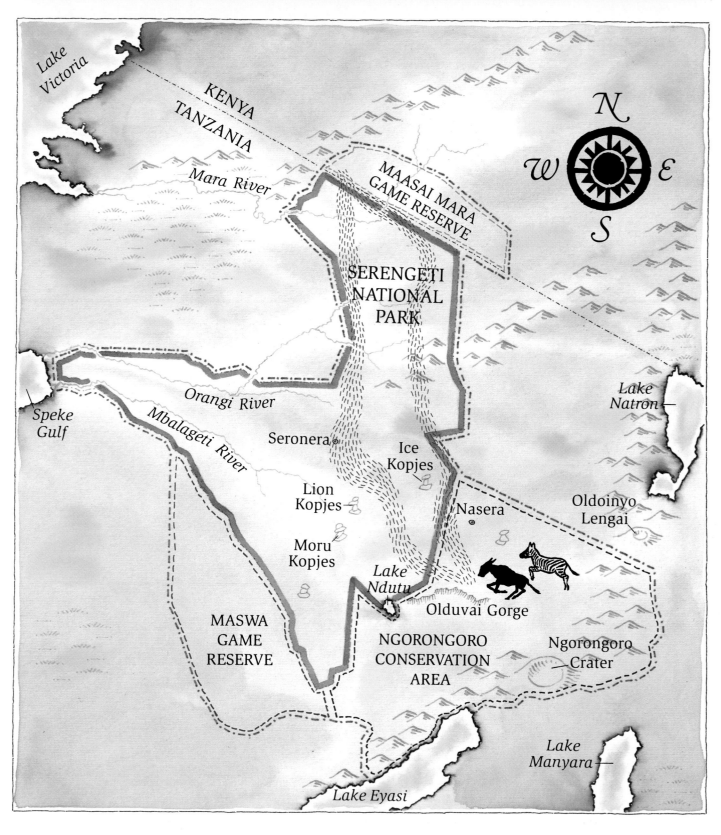

Lake Victoria

KENYA
TANZANIA

Mara River

MAASAI MARA
GAME RESERVE

SERENGETI
NATIONAL
PARK

N
W E
S

Lake
Natron

Orangi River

Speke
Gulf

Mbalageti River

Seronera

Ice
Kopjes

Lion
Kopjes

Nasera

Oldoinyo
Lengai

Moru
Kopjes

Lake
Ndutu

Olduvai Gorge

MASWA
GAME
RESERVE

NGORONGORO
CONSERVATION
AREA

Ngorongoro
Crater

Lake
Manyara

Lake Eyasi

Scale in Miles

0   10   20   30   40   50

Imagine one and a half million wildebeests—large antelopes with cowlike horns and long, wispy beards—and 750,000 zebras galloping together in search of green grass to eat and fresh water to drink. The force of those nine million hooves pounding the earth and causing the ground to shudder would make you feel as though you were in the middle of an earthquake.

A zebra's stripes are thought to help in its defense. The mass of vertical and horizontal stripes of a running herd *(right)* confuses a predator and makes it difficult to see where each individual animal begins and ends.

Wildebeests *(below)* are motivated by a herd instinct. They blindly follow one another on their perilous seven-hundred-mile migratory journey.

Each year these two massive herds undertake an awe-inspiring seven-hundred-mile journey through the Serengeti National Park. The Serengeti—East Africa's first national park, created in 1941—comprises 5,600 square miles of bush, woodlands, grassy plains, and riverine forests and is home to hundreds of species of wildlife. What is truly special about the Serengeti and what inspired the government of Tanzania to protect it is the Serengeti migration—one of the most dramatic spectacles in the world. The migration, which follows a circular route and takes nine months to complete, is a dangerous trek. The animals must cross lakes and rushing rivers, give birth, and risk their young to predators—lions, leopards, cheetahs, wild dogs, and hyenas—that follow them every step of the way.

When grass is plentiful the herds of zebras and wildebeests *(above right)* mingle together, spread out across the landscape.

Lionesses *(below right)* are the hunters of the pride (a group of lions), often working together in order to kill more effectively.

For many years it was believed that hyenas *(left)* survived by scavenging off kills made by others. Studies now show that hyenas kill as efficiently as lions or wild dogs. Hunting in packs, they are capable of pulling down a full-grown buffalo.

The journey begins just outside the southeastern border of the Serengeti near a dried-up riverbed named Olduvai Gorge. The wildebeests and zebras gather to feed on the new grasses brought by the torrential showers of the rainy season, which usually occurs in January. Slowly the animals make their way west into the park.

Nearly two million years ago early human beings roamed the plains of East Africa and settled around a lake that is now a dried-up riverbed called Olduvai Gorge *(right)*. Their stone tools can still be found buried among the rocks.

The rainy season is heralded by towering black clouds *(below)* that burst with immense force. The rain pours down in columns, often leaving the land not directly under the cloud unchanged and dry.

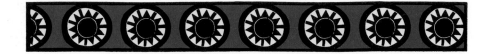

The southern Serengeti—a dust bowl with barely a hint of sun-parched grass in the dry season—turns into a lush, green pasture overnight. Delicate yellow flowers blanket the plains, and clear pools of fresh water collect. The pungent smell of wet earth hangs in the still air.

After just a few days of rain the grass turns from parched brown to lush green, and wildflowers cover the plains.

Male impalas *(left)* are distinguished from the females by the slender, curved horns that they use for fighting. As well as using these horns to fend off attackers, the impalas use them to fight each other for territory and to gain control of a harem of females.

The ostrich *(right)* is the largest, heaviest, and fastest-running bird in the world and has the largest eye of any land animal. Its wings are not used for flying; they act as stabilizers when the ostrich runs and as parasols to protect its young from the tropical sun.

The short-grass plains of the south are the herds' favorite feeding grounds and the place where they give birth. Alongside the wildebeests and zebras a great number of impalas, gazelles, elands, ostriches, topis, and hartebeests gather there to graze. They soon exhaust the supply of grass and move north in search of greener pastures. This constant onward motion in search of food is the essence of migration.

Large animals such as elephants and buffaloes eat the coarsest, tallest grasses, clearing the way for the migration through the plains. By eating the chest-high grasses, they leave behind a pasture where fine, leafier grasses can sprout. It is these grasses that the wildebeests and zebras eat. In turn, as the wildebeests and zebras move on, leaving even finer grasses, other animals follow behind to feed. This progression of animals is called the grazing sequence.

In order for an elephant to have such beautiful, long tusks *(above right)* it must reach old age. Today this is very rare because many elephants are killed by poachers when still young.

Cape buffaloes *(below right)* travel in mixed breeding herds of males and females, in small all-male groups of old bulls, or alone. They usually avoid the open plains and graze instead in the bush, where they can find shade as well as water to wallow in.

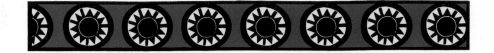

When the wildebeests and zebras are grazing on the short-grass plains they are so thickly spread across the landscape that, from a distance, it looks as if the earth itself is flowing like a river. As the grass is consumed or withers from lack of rain, the animals turn northwest toward the long-grass plains. Beautifully muscled and striped, the zebras lead the migration off the short-grass plains. Clustered in knots, then stretched out in ribbons, the wildebeests follow.

Although the gray whale's migration is seventeen times longer, the zebra's and wildebeest's migration is the most crowded and dangerous of any in the world.

18

The herds reach the long-grass plains near Seronera, in the center of the park, in late May, as the dry season begins. Elephants and buffaloes have passed through already and left behind the tender grasses for the wildebeests and zebras to eat. The herds wind around huge outcrops of shaped and balanced rocks called kopjes. They graze with skittish wariness because predators lurk in the shadows.

Even though the lionesses do most of the hunting, male lions always eat the kill first *(above right)*, leaving what's left for the females and cubs.

Natural formations of boulders such as these look like huge modern sculptures atop one another at Moru Kopjes *(below right)*.

Seronera is a well-watered section of the Serengeti famous for its fever trees *(left)*. Fever trees are so called because they grow in mosquito-breeding areas. Yellow fever is a deadly disease that is caused by the bite of an infected mosquito.

Smooth and rounded from centuries of weather, kopjes are literally islands of rock in a sea of grass. Some of them pierce the earth as one giant block; others, such as Moru Kopjes, tumble in cracked and broken piles over miles of plains. They are home to an array of vegetation and wildlife—some found nowhere else in the Serengeti—and provide shade and pools of water.

Nasera Rock offers browsers—such as the giraffe—an abundance of trees with delicate leaves on which to feed. While the giraffe is best known for its lengthy neck, its legs are among its most important assets. They are exceptionally long and muscular and can kick with a force that makes even a lion think twice about attacking.

Baboons are the most visible of the kopje inhabitants because they scale the rocks in their search for fruit and seeds. Hyraxes, small squirrellike animals with a shrill, piercing call, are the most audible. Puff adders, spitting cobras, and pancake tortoises—whose shape allows them to slip into rock crevices—all live in the kopjes.

While a baboon eats wild fruit on the sun-warmed face of Nasera Rock *(above right)*, it must always remain alert to the threat of a swooping eagle or a stalking leopard.

The rock hyrax *(below right)*, an inhabitant of the Serengeti kopjes, rarely emerges before sunrise, when it will sunbathe for a couple of hours before seeking shelter from hot midday temperatures. During this time the rock hyrax is especially vulnerable to predators.

A baboon troop *(left)* consists of between thirty and a hundred members. They live primarily on a diet of roots, grass, fruit, and insects, but they will also hunt and kill young impalas and other small antelopes.

The more inaccessible reaches of the kopjes are nesting sites for birds of prey such as the perfectly camouflaged spotted eagle owl, which swoops down on hares and hyraxes from its lofty perch. Cheetahs, leopards, and lions seek out the kopjes for solitude, protection for their young, and strategic hunting advantage.

As the dry season intensifies, the plains' water sources dry up and the grasses wither, causing the herds to move on again. The zebras and wildebeests wind northward toward the bush and the woodlands, where permanent rivers and shrubs hardy enough to survive the lack of rain can sustain them.

One advantage the spotted eagle owl *(above right)* depends on when hunting is its perfect camouflage, which makes it all but invisible on the speckled gray rocks.

When absolutely still, a lioness *(below right)* is virtually impossible to see in the kopjes. She uses this camouflage and the good view from the high rocks to successfully stalk her prey.

In the northern Serengeti the landscape changes from open grasslands to thorny shrubs and thickening bush. Grazers, such as gazelles, stay behind, while browsers, such as giraffes and black rhinoceroses, which eat leafy shrubs and trees, move forward. The bush becomes woodland at the Serengeti's northern boundary, and throughout the woodlands permanent rivers flow.

The black rhinoceros is one of two types of African rhinoceros, the other one being the white rhinoceros. All species of rhino are nearly extinct. Rhinoceroses are greatly threatened by poachers, who kill them for their horns and skins. In an effort to increase the population of black rhinos, some have been sent to Australia and the United States to form breeding colonies for future repopulation of their native environment.

Lining the river courses are majestic mahogany and fig trees, where many species of birds make their nests. Elephants also take refuge in the woodlands, where they can satisfy their gargantuan feeding needs: three hundred pounds of food and fifty gallons of water a day for each one.

Even with grasses and water more plentiful, however, the wildebeests and zebras are eager to move on. Here the threat they sense does not come from their traditional enemies, such as lions and hyenas, but from human beings. Not far from the herds' migration route on the northern boundary of the Serengeti are human settlements—permanent villages as well as temporary campsites. Some of the people who live in these settlements have turned to poaching—illegally hunting animals for meat, horns, and skins—as their means of living. Every year thousands of animals are killed—wildebeests for their meat, zebras for their skins, and elephants for their tusks. Other animals for which there is no market often become accidentally trapped in the snares and are killed as well.

A young elephant will stay with its family for almost fifteen years as it learns how to forage for food and protect itself.

After a hard rain the Mara River is transformed from a peaceful, meandering watercourse into a rushing current *(left)*, making it all the more difficult for the herds to cross.

In August the herds warily make their way through the woodlands to the banks of the wide Mara River. Faced with rushing, swollen waters, the wildebeests and zebras must somehow cross to the grasslands beyond. With the herds behind creating intense pressure, they leap blindly at all angles. There is a mad scramble to survive in the thrashing water. Some paddle frantically and clamber up the muddy bank. Some land on the backs of others who drown. Most make it across, but by the end of the day countless numbers have been swept downriver into the jaws of waiting crocodiles. There the feeding frenzy is alive with snapping, snarling, and hissing, but so many bodies collect there that, even after the crocodiles and scavenging hyenas, jackals, and vultures have satisfied their appetites, many half-eaten carcasses are left behind.

Crocodiles wait in the Mara River *(right)* for the herds of wildebeests and zebras to attempt to cross. Because the reptiles are so adept in the water, a mammal has very little chance of surviving an attack in the river.

Hippopotamuses *(left)* walk along river bottoms, such as the Mara's, and can stay underwater for as long as six minutes. Despite their round, heavy body and short legs, hippos are excellent swimmers and can run as fast as a human being.

While the hartebeest, wildebeest, and zebra herds like to graze in the long-grass plains *(below)*, they are wary of lions and cheetahs that can stalk them, unseen.

On the opposite side of the river, calm returns, and the surviving wildebeests and zebras enjoy a new supply of abundant grass. Depending on where the rains have fallen most heavily and, consequently, where green grass and water are still plentiful, the herds will cross and recross the Mara River in their search for food.

Throughout the last three months of their migratory cycle, the herds once again travel across the face of the Serengeti National Park, leaving in their wake a ravaged landscape, scattered bones, and rutted tracks dug by millions of hooves. In November they head southward, back toward Olduvai Gorge, where they disperse, looking for patches of grass and surviving pools of water until the next rainy season begins.

Clouds of dust obscure the running herds of zebras and wildebeests *(right)* as they move on to greener pastures.

The migrating wildebeest and zebra herds are a movable feast for predators. Wildebeest skulls *(left)* lying on the shore of Lake Ndutu are all that remain of a kill.

GLOSSARY

Browsers

Animals such as giraffes that have delicate snouts and feed on leaves, flowers, and shrubs, often carefully selecting and eating just one leaf at a time. The browse line is the neat line on the underside of trees that have been meticulously pruned by a browser.

Bush

A type of habitat in which thick shrubbery covers between 15 percent and 20 percent of the ground.

Camouflage

The markings and colorings on an animal's coat that enable it to blend with its surroundings. Camouflage is an effective means of hiding from predators as well as from prey.

Grassland

A nearly treeless expanse of land where various types of grasses grow. The African grasslands support the highest concentration of large mammals in the world. Also known in Africa as savanna.

Grazers

Animals such as wildebeests and zebras that have wide snouts and feed on grass.

Grazing Sequence

The order in which various species of animals migrate across a particular piece of land.

Habitat

The natural home of a plant or animal.

Herd

A number of wild animals of the same kind that congregate together.

Kopje

An Afrikaans word meaning "small head" used to describe outcrops of very old granite in the Serengeti grasslands. Many of the kopjes—such as Lion Kopjes and Ice Kopjes—are so named either for the animals that live there or for their appearance.

Long-Grass Plain

A type of grassland characterized by tall grasses that grow as high as a zebra's back.

Migration

The process wherein animals periodically pass from one region or climate to another for feeding or breeding.

Poaching

The illegal practice of killing animals for meat, skins, ivory, or trophies. In most cases the poacher (a person who poaches) sells the animal by-products for a profit.

Riverine Forest

A forest that lines a river. The Serengeti's riverine forests are composed mostly of acacia, fig, and mahogany trees.

Short-Grass Plain

A type of grassland characterized by short grasses that wither in the dry season and by the lack of any permanent water supplies such as lakes, springs, or rivers.

Woodland

A type of habitat in which trees cover more than 20 percent of the ground.

Author's Note

Although *The Serengeti Migration* is a book about the animals of the Serengeti, people have lived in and been an integral part of preserving the Serengeti long before the government of Tanzania declared it a national park. Throughout time the Serengeti has been home to many different groups of people. One of these groups–the Maasai–lived there until recently. For more than two hundred years, the Maasai traveled over the land, moving from the short-grass to the long-grass plains, herding cattle, sheep, and goats. Much like the wildebeests and zebras, they moved in a cycle that was controlled by the rains, looking for green grass and fresh water for their herds.

The Maasai call the Serengeti *Sirenket,* which in their language means "the place where the eye never ends." *Sirenket* is their culture's vision of paradise–their promised land. Generation after generation of Maasai children have been told stories of encounters with lions in the Serengeti, of floods and droughts that destroyed precious grazing land, and of violent eruptions of fire and ash from *Oldoinyo Lengai,* or Mountain of God–the only active volcano in East Africa.

Although the Maasai now live outside the Serengeti National Park, these stories and the traditions born of the land help them to remember that the Serengeti was once theirs to roam freely. And we should never forget that they were once a vital part of this breath-taking environment.